Business Success Techniques
Your Guide to Profitability

By

David K. Ewen, M.Ed.

Forest Academy

ISBN-13: 978-1492712183
ISBN-10: 1492712183

This book represents slides from business training created by

Forest Academy

www.ForestAcademy.org

Business Success Techniques
Your Guide To Profitability
By
David K. Ewen, M.Ed.
Forest Academy
www.ForestAcademy.org

ISBN-13: 978-1492712183

ISBN-10: 1492712183

Agenda Topics

1. Introduction To Business
2. Types of Businesses
3. Forms to Create Business
4. Health Care Options
5. Certification and License
6. Business Plan Document
7. Fundraising and Building Cash
8. Understanding Your Customers
9. Getting Paid by Credit Card
10. Marketing Elements
11. WIIFM describing "WHY"
12. RASCIL describing "WHO" & "WHAT"
13. The 5 W's to describe your business
14. Rewards & Incentives
15. Media Publicity Delivery & Channels
16. Communication Tools
17. Business Cycles & Financial Conditions
18. Financial Statements

The Business

Forms of Businesses

Sole Proprietorship - A sole proprietor is someone who owns an unincorporated business by himself or herself.

Limited Liability Company (LLC) - Either declared a partnership or corporation. (typically an S Corporation).

Corporation - The profit of a corporation is taxed to the corporation when earned, and then is taxed to the shareholders when distributed as dividends. This creates a double tax. The corporation does not get a tax deduction when it distributes dividends to shareholders. Shareholders cannot deduct any loss of the corporation.

Class S Corporation or S Corporation - S corporations are corporations that elect to pass corporate income, losses, deductions and credit through to their shareholders for federal tax purposes. Shareholders of S corporations report the flow-through of income and losses on their personal tax returns and are assessed tax at their individual income tax rates. This allows S corporations to avoid double taxation on the corporate income. S corporations are responsible for tax on certain built-in gains and passive income.

Check out the official videos from the IRS. `http://www.irsvideos.gov/SmallBusinessTaxpayer/StartingaBusiness`

Necessary Forms

As a corporation, the state needs to receive and sign off on an "Articles of Organization". The fees and forms are different for each state.   Basicly it dictates name, function, bylaws, and titles for President, Secretary, and Treasurer.

The businesses needs it's own "social security number" for tax purposes if it is not a sole proprietorship. This is called an EIN. Employer identification number. The form to file is: **SS-4** (search in www.irs.gov). It is filed after receiving approval and signoff from the state for your articles of organization.

If you filed as a non-profit corporation and want to file for tax exemption.   The form to file is: **Form 1023** (search in www.irs.gov)

To operate in a town/city you may be required to file a business certificate with your city/town hall within your state

If you are not incorporated and operating as a sole proprietorship, then a business certificate must be filed with your town/city hall

Do you want help forming a company? Go to **www.incorporate.com**   David Ewen is not associated with the Corporation Company. This company is offered as a suggestion for assistance.

Health Insurance

There is not one definitive universal answer that traverses intrastate.

The best option is to have a phone call with a local insurance broker to discuss options. The legal requirements change year-to-year.

Many startups have a spouse with insurance or work part time to benefit from insurance.

To ensure you are legally compliant in health care coverage and supporting your needs, go to the link from the Small Business Association.

www.sba.gov/content/health-care
www.healthcare.gov

Keep up to date: **www.whitehouse.gov/healthreform**

Certification and Licence

There are businesses that have the requirement that owners and employees need to be licensed and / or certified to operate. Is that true for your business? If so what kind of training or education is needed to finally become certified or licensed? Every business is different, so as a business owner, you need to determine the requirements.

If you need help determining what your business needs, here are potential resources that may help you.

- www.SBA.gov - Small Business Assocation
- www.bbb.org - Better Business Bureau
- www.uschamber.com - US Chamber of Commerce

You can also go to your local chamber of commerce or seek a local trade association online.

Finally, you could just ask. Use the resources of social media to pose a question to receive direction.

Documenting The Business with a BUSINESS PLAN

Business Plan

A documented business is an organized business that is able to get funding from a variety of resources. This includes banks, grants, investors, and crowdfunding.

An organized business is successful. Business plans have the following contents:

- Cover Page
- Table of Contents
- Summary & Business Plan (objective, goal)
- Business Organization & Management (leaders, team members)
- Background (skills, training, experience)
- Marketing & Advertising Plan
- Action Plan (Development, Production)
- Financial Statements (bank, accounting)
- Contracts (lease, licenses, agreements)
- Appendix (resume, market statistics)

Business Plan Thoughts

- Cover Page
- Table of Contents
- **Summary & Business Plan (objective, goal)**
  - What are the lines of business?
  - Who are the customers?
  - How are the customer's served?
- **Business Organization & Management (leaders, team members)**
  - Who's the boss?
  - Who are the helpers?
  - Are there outsourced contractors?
- **Background (skills, training, experience)**
  - What is it that makes the business capable?
  - What do you look for in an employee?
- **Marketing & Advertising Plan**
  - How will your customers learn about you?
  - How do you plan to grow your customer base?
- **Action Plan (Development, Production)**
  - What are the start up efforts?
  - How will you keep the momentum of the business going?
  - How will you adapt to economic conditions & technology trends?
- Financial Statements (bank, accounting)
- Contracts (lease, licenses, agreements)
- Appendix (resume, market statistics)

Fundraising Efforts & Building Cash

Funding

Source for finding and applying for Federal Grants **www.Grants.gov**

Small Business Startup Loans **www.SBA.gov** (small business association)

Training & Education **http://studentaid.ed.gov**

Other Federal Government Benefits (to help offset costs) **www.Benefits.gov**

Crowdfunding: Donations generated from reward incentives that are paid online.

- GoFundMe.com
- Indiegogo.com
- KickStarter.com
- PeerBackers.com
- WeFunder.com

Reward incentive could be ownership or stock in the company.   Other incentives could be as simple as a t-shirt.

Crowdfunding

In the past, only accredited investors were legally able to invest in startups as a tax writeoff. These people were typically the wealthy. They had to document their knowledge of the industry and the ability of the newly formed company was able to absorb potential losses.

Jobs Act signed by President Obama in April 2012 to take effect in January 2013 allowing anyone to invest in a startup company regardless of wealth with no formal accreditation process. This will help fuel investments for new small companies.

Learn more by searching for "**Jobs Act Crowdfunding**".

Crowdfunding

The two major crowdfunding websites are:

- www.KickStarter.com
- www.IndieGoGo.com

Others include:

- http://www.rockethub.com
- http://www.gofundme.com

Easy Fundraising On Facebook & Email

You can create an easy fundraising site to share on social media in less than five minutes

Create an account on **www.YouCaring.com** (totally free) and post your project link in Facebook. Have Facebook friends share the link.

Create an email chain that shares your YouCaring project.

Fundraising Without Car Washes

Everyone loves to save money. A coupon book is sold to customers. The advertisers pay for it. Value Book Publishing prints it. You sell it to make a profit.

http://ValueBookPublishing.com

Sell Products To Raise Funds

There are lots of products to sell to help raise funds.   Here is a place to select from a variety of fundraising products.

http://www.FundRaiserSuperStore.com

Understanding Your Customers

Funnel of Customers

There is the notion of filling the Funnel when understanding customer traffic.

New customers come in while old customers become obsolete and bleed off. In the middle you have the core. **80% of your business comes from 20% of your customers**. The remaining bulk of your customer is the fluid coming in and going out. The business process of clamping off the bleed is called retaining or customer retention.

The important thing in this discussion is to be aware of the bleed of customers and be conscious of the need to always fill the funnel.

The core group of customers need to be retained. There's a cost of associated with acquiring new customers. It's an additional cost to keep the customers. Keep this in mind when you are working with word-of-mouth advertising, referrals, reward incentives, and loyalty bonuses.

Types of Customers

Buyers come in three categories. Those who <u>need</u>, <u>want</u>, or <u>avoid</u>. What kind of buyers do you attract?

- **Need**: Purchase to satisfy a requirement.
- **Want**: Desire to have, but not a necessity
- **Avoid**: Will purchase to avoid a consequence of not buying

What kind of service or product are you providing for each category of customer? Might you be missing a category? How can your plan to support all categories?

Do Customers Listen To You?

In general, people remember 40% of what you tell them. It is natural an and expected. This means about 60% is forgotten.

As a business owner you won't know what your customer or client will remember you told them. You will know that they will forget most of it.

Be aware of that and give your customers the tools to help remember your message. Make follow up phone calls to check on satisfaction and understanding. Mail a thank you card or appreciation card in the mail.

Try using visual aids:

- Your business card with a website
- Colorful brochures
- A reminder card for appointments
- Coupons as incentive to come back

Selling To Customer

There are many methods of selling to a customer and convincing them you have the best product or service. It boils down to features and benefits. You'll do better by distinguishing between the two.

Features Tell **&** Benefits Sell

- A feature for a new car is power door locks. The benefit is fast easy access.

- A feature might be a the walk-in-closet. The benefit is space / organization.

- A feature of a new chair is the cushion seat. The benefit is comfort.

Customer Education

Your customers are regular everyday people with the same learning skills as anyone else. You want your customers to learn about you in the simplest easy to understand way.

People learn in one or a combination of three ways. The are:

- **Tell:** People learn by listening and being told
- **Show:** People learn by observing and being shown
- **Do:** People that learn by doing and taking hands on approach

What can you do to teach your customers about your product or service? In what ways can you tell them, show them, and have them do something to learn?

With current technology

(1) How can a website or blog help? Can this be interactive?
(2) How can a business card or brochure help?
(3) How can a radio interview or online video help?
(4) In what venues can you do a demonstration?

Getting Paid

Accept Credit Card Payments

PayPal (**www.PayPal.com**) is the online tool to have funds emailed to your PayPal account where you can then transfer to your bank account. You can also maintain funds in your PayPal and make use of the funds with your PayPal debit account. The debit account is managed with a Mastercard or Visa card.

You can create a simple blog using **www.Blogger.com** from Google and accept secure credit card payments on your blog. If you have a web site, you can do the same there. Your business card will have your blog or website so your customer's know where to go. Quality business cards can be made at Vista Print (**www.VistaPrint.com**)

If you you have direct access to a customer, you can accept credit card payments with a card swipe device attached to your cell phone. This costs 2.75% per transaction and done through Square Up at **www.SquareUp.com** There are no additional fees and you can enjoy next day deposits. You can accept Visa, Mastercard, Discover, and American Express. This works with iOS and Android devices. *PayPal now offers this same type of service. Take advantage of both.*

Marketing

Marketing

This is the formula to represent yourself. It's easy to explain, but very hard to do.

- WIIFM = (It/This) will (Make/Give) you __(why?/passion)__
- RASCIL = Reliability, Authenticity, Simplicity, Completeness, Illustration, Location
- 5 W's = Who, What, When, Where, Why

Together, they have a combined formula / Copyright (c) 2012, David K. Ewen, M.Ed.

Who

What ├─── Who & What = RASCIL

When .... Time frame

Where .... Location

Why = WIIFM

WIIFM

WIIFM is What's In It For Me

WIIFM = (It/This) will (Make/Give) you __(why?/passion)__

Some examples are:

- It will make you happy
- This will make you successful
- It will give you chills
- This will give you love

WIIFM represents the

- Passion
- Why
- Result
- Impact

WIIFM - Common Mistakes

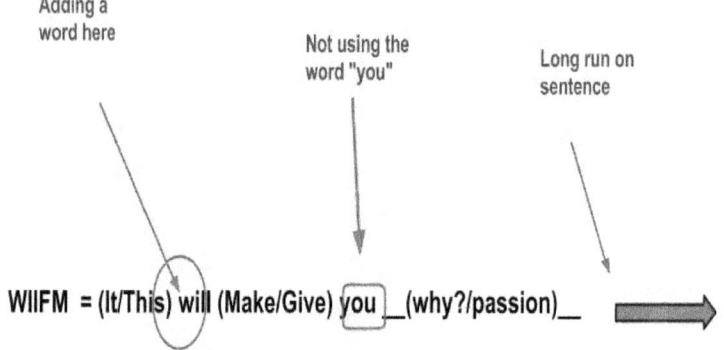

Adding a
word here

Not using the
word "you"

Long run on
sentence

WIIFM = (It/This) will (Make/Give) you __(why?/passion)__

WIIFM - Intent of Formula

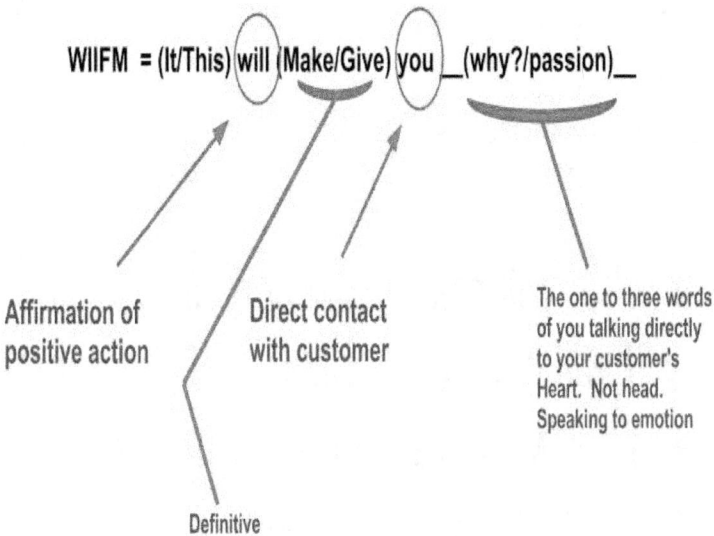

WIIFM = (It/This) will (Make/Give) you __(why?/passion)__

Affirmation of positive action

Direct contact with customer

The one to three words of you talking directly to your customer's Heart. Not head. Speaking to emotion

Definitive

Example: WIIFM

Scary Book from Stephen King

WIIFM = (It/This) will (Make/Give) you __ Emotion / Impact __

- This will make you scream
- It will give you chills
- This will give you nightmares
- It will make you shiver

RASCIL

RASCIL represent the WHO & WHAT. It is to be used as a general guide to help ensure facts aren't missed.

The origin of RASCIL is the design of yellow page ads

- R = Reliability   Length of service / longevity
- A = Authenticity   Certificates, licenses, degrees, accolades
- S = Simplicity   Easy access to your product or service
- C = Completeness   Different lines of business & channels of customers
- I = Illustration   Logo or overall look
- L = Location   How are you contacted? Address? Phone? Email? Website?

Use an example of a family owned auto mechanic garage in the yellow pages.

- R = Reliability   ... Since 1976
- A = Authenticity   ... ACE Certified
- S = Simplicity   ... Early drop off, weekend hours
- C = Completeness   ... oil change, mufflers, auto body repair, tires
- I = Illustration   ... Picture of clean garage with tools hanging neatly
- L = Location   ... Address, phone

RASCIL

RASCIL represent the WHO & WHAT. It is to be used as a general guide to help ensure facts aren't missed.

The origin of RASCIL is the design of yellow page ads

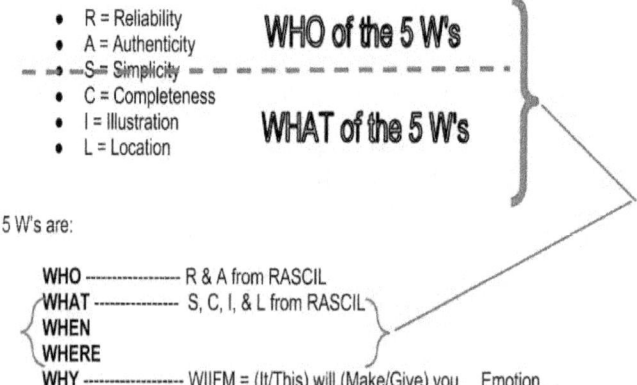

- R = Reliability
- A = Authenticity   **WHO of the 5 W's**
- S = Simplicity
- C = Completeness
- I = Illustration   **WHAT of the 5 W's**
- L = Location

5 W's are:

WHO ---------------- R & A from RASCIL
WHAT --------------- S, C, I, & L from RASCIL
WHEN
WHERE
WHY ---------------- WIIFM = (It/This) will (Make/Give) you __Emotion__

5 W's

Tying it all together. WIIFM & RASCIL combine with the 5 W's to make your marketing content

- WIIFM = (It/This) will (Make/Give) you __(Why?/Passion)__
- RASCIL = **R**eliability, **A**uthenticity, **S**implicity, **C**ompleteness, Illustration, Location
- 5 W's = Who, What, When, Where, Why

Together, they have a combined formula / Copyright (c) 2012, David K. Ewen, M.Ed.

Who

What   Who & What = RASCIL

When .... Time frame

Where .... Location

Why = WIIFM

Using 5 W's

Example of Cardiologist writing a book about eating healthy

- WHO   Dr. David Ewen
- WHAT   Wrote a book about eating healthy
- WHEN   There will be a book signing next week
- WHERE   Signing at Barnes & Noble
- WHY   It will make you feel great

Same book, but described in another way

- WHO   Award winning cardiologist
- WHAT   The need to eat healthy
- WHEN   It's never too late
- WHERE   All across America
- WHY   This will give you good health

Remember

- WHEN is any type of Time Frame
- WHERE is any type of Location

Tying It All Together

This is the formula to represent yourself. It's easy to explain, but very hard to do.

- WIIFM = (It/This) will (Make/Give) you __(Why?/Passion)__
- RASCIL = **R**eliability, **A**uthenticity, **S**implicity, **C**ompleteness, **I**llustration, **L**ocation
- 5 W's = Who, What, When, Where, Why

Together, they have a combined formula / Copyright (c) 2012, David K. Ewen, M.Ed.

Who

What ⊢ Who & What = RASCIL

When .... Time frame

Where .... Location

Why = WIIFM

Learn more by ordering this book at
Amazon or Barnes and Noble

- www.Amazon.com
- www.BN.com

Publicity Made Simple
Success With Media Relations

By:

David K. Ewen, M.Ed.

Rewards
&
Incentives
(part of WIIFM)

Satisfying Customer With Rewards & Incentives

As part of your marketing campaign and publicity, you want to give the customer rewards for loyalty and incentives for doing business. Today this is what steers customers from one business venue to another. It has been effective for many years and in today's economic climate used even more. Examples are:

- High volume purchases result in bulk discount
- First time buyer receives discount coupon for subsequent purchase within 30 days
- Frequent purchases demonstrating loyalty is rewarded with free membership constant discounts

The discounts and coupons are typically in the area of **15% off** of the normal price.

Make sure all brochures and flyers have the following:

(1) Bulk discount rate of single one time purchases.
(2) Clip out coupon after 1st purchase with expiration date.
(3) Customer reward program or Loyalty program recognizing frequent purchases

Media

Publicity

Talk Show Circuit

www.Radio-Locator.com

Search for radio
shows by zip code.

Great opportunity to
tour the country using
the phone at home.

Internet Radio

The shows from internet radio are saved as podcasts. The links to saved shows can be shared on social media sites and email marketing. Find the best shows for you to reach out to.

- www.BlogTalkRadio.com
- www.Spreaker.com
- www.Live365.com
- www.VoiceAmerica.com

Feature Article

An author can be nicely represented in a feature article. Send a news release out.

- www.Examiner.com
- www.AllVoices.com
- Voices.Yahoo.com
- www.HubPages.com
- Also, local newspapers

Share the feature article on social media (facebook, twitter, etc.)

Social Media

Take advantage of networking with your readers and fellow authors.

- www.Facebook.com
- www.Twitter.com
- LinkedIn
- www.MySpace.com
- You can find others

Share links from your feature articles and radio shows

Broadcast TV & Radio

You can take advantage of your local mainstream broadcast media.   They all have websites with contact information.

(1) Email a news release using the 5 W's with RASCIL and WIIFM

(2) Print the email, and mail it

(3) Place your event on their website community calendar.

(4) Be available to answer the phone immediately

(5) Position your event near the TV or radio station so reporters don't have to travel.

(6) Do the same with newspapers.

Communication

Communication Tools

Website
- The easiest alternative for a web site is a blog. If nothing else, have a blog.
- GOOGLE provides blogs, phone number with voice mail, and email address
- Go to www.Blogger.com - Your blog will be   __your-ID__.BlogSpot.com
- If you are relatively tech savy, create a free web site from www.Webs.com and register a domain name from www.GoDaddy.com or www.Register.com and foward the domain name (URL) to the web site you created on www.webs.com

Email address
- To set up your email address: http://mail.google.com
- Download the Google mail app to your smartphone or tablet and access your email anytime.

Phone number
- To set up a telephone that has voice mail & forwarded (optional) to your cell is http://voice.google.com

Calendar
- Create a calendar and set up email invites and reminders by going to http://Calendar.Google.com.

Business Cards, Postcards, brochures.
- Put your email, phone, blog, web site on your business card, postcard, etc.
- www.VistaPrint.com - 250 free business cards (ongoing promo - has vistaprint on the back)

Revenue Portal

Web and mobile applications make it easier for customers to pay you for products and services.

(1) Take advantage of **PayPal** and **Square** (Square UP) to receive payments on your cell phone with a card swipe attachment.

(2) Send invoices by email and receive payment by email

(3) Receive online payments and access through debit card or transfer to your bank.

(4) Both PayPal and Square are competing in similar markets so it is likely that other companies providing similar services will pop up.

Learn more by going to www.PayPal.com and www.SquareUp.com

Business Cycles

Financing

Ratio = Equity / Debt

If equity is higher than debt, the ratio is > 1 (a number in the form of one point *blah, blah*)

If equity is less than debt, the ratio is < 1 (a number in the form of zero point *blah, blah*)

Lenders are looking for an equity/debt ratio greater than one. In other words the value of equity is much greater than the value of debt. This would demonstrate collateral.

Basic Financial Statements

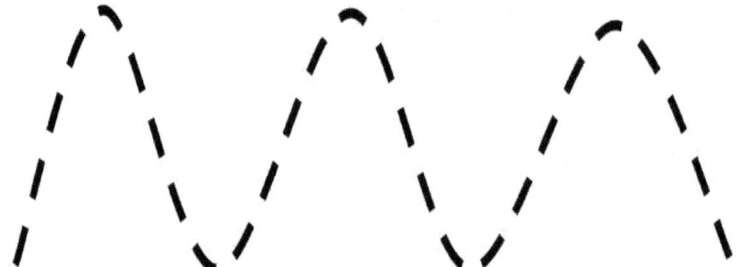

The income of a business goes through peaks and valleys. A landscaping business is busy during the summer and quiet during the winter. Looking at the bank activity in the past you can see that. The current bank statement shows where you are in the cycle. You can predict future trending if given enough bank activity in the past to make a prediction. This prediction allows you to plan for the future.

If a landscaping business knows from its bank activity that its quiet during the winter and verifies that by seeing bank statements each January, then they know to make a change. A diversified approach would make that business perhaps put a plow in front of the truck to add snow clearing during the quiet times of landscaping. Trending will change and result in a more smoothed out diagram showing the peaks and valleys of the business.

Slow Times of Business

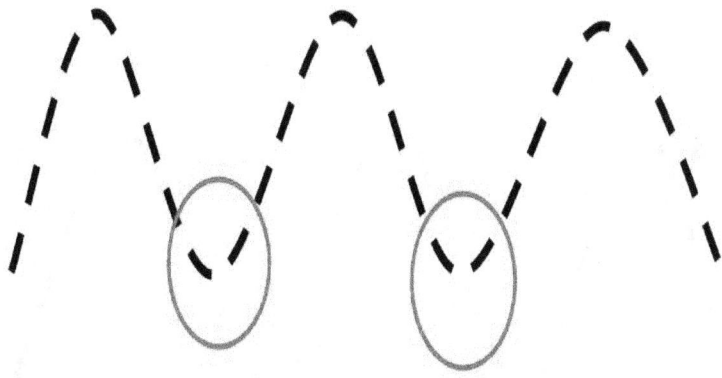

The past bank activity and current bank statement can help you prepare for the slow down times in the future. You can predict when the slow times can be. Be aware and know that a diversified business can have alternate lines of business to pick up the slow times.

Good Happy Times of Business

When income activity is high during seasonal high volume, this is the time to:

(1) Save money for slow down time
(2) Spend on R.O.I. vehicles (R.O.I. = Return on Investment)
      a. Equipment/software/tools that will produce more & save money in the future
      b. Advertising to increase customer volume during slow times

Organizing & Planning Finances

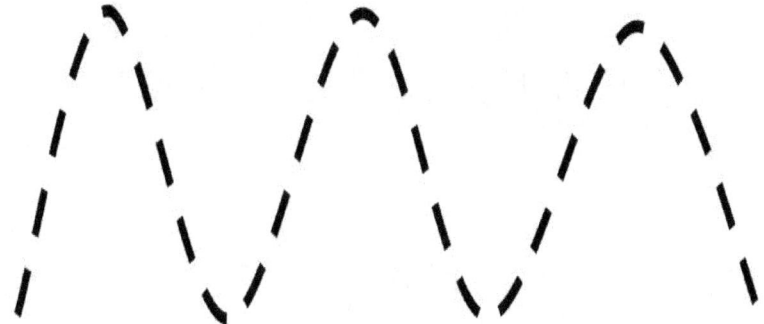

The best way to predict accurately the future trends of a business is to look at a graphical representation of the actual numbers for income and expenses of a business over a few years of operation. Business survive because of the honest, dedicated analysis of numbers. It doesn't have to be hard. All you need to do is to track the past, know the present, and predict future trends.

Past is represented by bank activity seen in the monthly bank statements (deposits, vs. withdrawals). Present is represented by the current bank statement and your status (What is owed vs. owned). Future is represented by a predicted model based on the past and changes in planning.

There are statements that a business creates that represents the Past, Present, and Future

Basic Overview

Financial Statements

Basic Financial Statements

The basic financial statements give the condition of the company in the past, present, or future.

- Past = **Cash Flow Statement** - reports on actual trends in the past

- Present = **Balance Sheet** - reports on a point-in-time status of the company

- Future = **Profit & Loss Statement** - reports on a projected forecast of the future

The simplest way to generate these types of reports is with Microsoft Excel.   Basically, there are pluses and minuses that will be calculated.   If you are savvy enough with excel, you can generate a graph, plot, or bar chart based on the reporting.   You can also use Quicken as your financial reporting tool.

Successful businesses focus on the tracking of income & expenses.   They do better by understanding trends to head off potential shortfalls and financial disasters.

Cash Flow Statement

Each budget item over a 3 month period has income and expenses.   For EACH month you'll have line items associated with Revenue and Expenses.

Revenue Itemized

    Month one
    .
    .
    Month two
    .
    .
    Month three
    .
    .
    TOTAL REVENUE = __#___

Total Income =
Total Expense =
Net Balance Over Period =

Expenses Itemized

    Month one
    .
    .
    Month two
    .
    .
    Month three
    .
    .
    TOTAL EXPENSE = __#___

Balance Sheet

The Balance Sheet reports on the status of a company on a specific day or point-in-time.

Remember the equation as "ALEO". / A=L+OE / Assets = Liability + Owner's Equity

Examples:

	Asset	Liability	Owner's Equity
• Today	Cut Grass	Payroll owed	Zero, $0.00
• Tomorrow	Same cut grass	$0.00	Paid payroll

	Asset	Liability	Owner's Equity
• Today	Tractor	$3000	Zero, $0.00
• 5 Yrs later	Same Tractor	$0.00	$1000 (paid + depreciated value)

Profit & Loss Statement

Each projected budget item over a 3 month period has an associated income and expenses.   For EACH month you'll have line items associated with Revenue and Expenses.

Projected Revenue Itemized

Month one
-
-
Month two
-
-
Month three
-
-
TOTAL REVENUE = __#__

Projected Expenses Itemized

Month one
-
-
Month two
-
-
Month three
-
-
TOTAL EXPENSE = __#__

Projected Total Income =

Projected Total Expense =

Net Balance Projected =

Learn More

www.SBA.gov

Business.usa.gov

This book represents slides from business training created by

Forest Academy

www.ForestAcademy.org

Business Success Techniques
Your Guide To Profitability
By
David K. Ewen, M.Ed.
Forest Academy
www.ForestAcademy.org

ISBN-13: 978-1492712183

ISBN-10: 1492712183

www.ingramcontent.com/pod-product-compliance
Lightning Source LLC
Chambersburg PA
CBHW071627170526
45166CB00003B/1223